108 Ways
To Great Days

A JOURNEY THROUGH JOURNALING

Guru Singh

re™
re*evolution
b o o k s

ISBN: 1-4392-4794-3

Editor:
Kevin Hutchings

Art Director:
Michael ('Sat Pavan Singh') Newsom

Creative Design:
(*page & cover art*)
Michael ('Sat Pavan Singh') Newsom

Publisher:
re*evolution books
Los Angeles, California

Author:
Guru Singh

contact and info:
GSGlobalCommunity@gmail.com

DEDICATION

This book is dedicated to my Mother and Father — yogis far ahead of the time . . . and **Yogi Bhajan** — a Yogi for the time.

FOREWORD

Why 108?

As the ancient world grew through an evolutionary progression, there was a particular culture of consciousness that emerged from the more abundant regions of our planet. Here, without harsh conditions and competition to survive, time was used to develop the commonwealth for the common good. With this grace as a backdrop instead of struggle, amazing advancements in many areas took place — Higher math developed with discovering algebra and geometry, conscious cuisine developed alongside farming and botany, knowledge of weaving produced the finest fabrics, and traditional herbal medicine and acupuncture were born from the science of yoga and meditation. Within all this advancement, Vedic astrology and astronomy charted the subtler aspects of human relations to the Cosmos.

The Bhavisia Purana was one of the texts written by this Humanitarian culture of ancient India and the Middle East. It was authored five thousand years before the instruments were invented to prove its accuracy, but this mystical Sanskrit text described astro-scientific facts discovered through processes of deep meditation. They discovered that the distance between the earth and the sun is (near) **108** times the sun's diameter; the diameter of the sun is (near) **108** times the earth's diameter, and the distance between the earth and the moon is (near) **108** times the moon's diameter.
From these harmonic relations between the Earth, the Sun and the Moon, the number— **108** — became absolutely **sacred.**
All prayer-meditation necklaces (malas) were strung with **108** beads.
108 was determined to be the number of steps between *ordinary human consciousness* and the center-point of *enlightened human consciousness.*
For this reason we have designed this journal to have 108 distinct steps . . . work with it and enjoy ~ first the process — then the results.

Guru Singh

About the author

Guru Singh DD, mss, is a third generation yogi and teacher of Humanology and Kundalini Yoga and meditation. He is also a musician, composer, author, and Minister of Sikh Dharma with a Doctorate of Divinity. Most importantly to him however, he is a family man . . . with a base in Los Angeles, Seattle, and India, Guru Singh teaches throughout the world with his wife Guruperkarma Kaur. Together they have two children . . . a son Sopurkh and a daughter Hari Purkh.

Members of Guru Singh's family lived in India in the early 20th Century. This is where his Great-Aunt met Paramahansa Yogananda, author of *Autobiography of a Yogi*, in Calcutta in 1916. She studied and traveled with this spiritual master from India to America and served him until his passing in 1952. Guru Singh was born in Seattle in 1945 into this yogic household setting the foundation for a spiritual life from the age of zero.

In January of 1969, Guru Singh (then 23) met and began a thirty four year long daily study with The Master of Kundalini Yoga - **Yogi Bhajan.** Guru Singh, the first Westerner to wear the turban, began accompanying Yogi Bhajan as he taught at Universities, lecture halls, spiritual centers and Sikh Gurudwaras around the world.

As a minister, Guru Singh works with spiritual and religious leaders of nearly every faith, including the Dalai Lama on Seeds of Compassion and Sri Amma Bhagavan of Oneness University. He draws on his extensive musical background and knowledge of Sahaj Shabd (sound) therapy to offer a unique approach to counseling the natural human harmonies through meditation and applied sound. He is also involved with Dr. Dharma Khalsa and Dr. Andrew Newberg of the University of Pennsylvania School of Medicine, Department of Neuro-Theology, using medical imaging to measure dynamic brain function under the influence of meditation, mantra, and prayer.

Guru Singh is one of the Founding Directors of the **Miri Piri Academy**- an international boarding school (K – 12) in Amritsar, India. Here, students from around the world become global citizens and future leaders through an academic curriculum delivered with a spiritual focus. Serving on the boards of several fast growth companies, he is dedicated to transforming today's world of education, technology, media and community building.

Join Guru Singh at :

http://blog.gurusingh.com/ for the daily Inspirational Blessings; and
http://podcast.gurusingh.com/ for Podcasts of current lectures.
Find a collection of his mantra CDs at **http://music.gurusingh.com/**
Participate in building a strong global community at:
http://global.gurusingh.com/
. . . All connecting the over-arching vision and spiritual mission
. . . reaching humanity personally, while teaching globally.

Acknowledgments

Blessings and gratitude to all who have touched my life;
inspired me; taught me to be inspirational in my words and actions;
enabled me to see through enthusiastic eyes;
given me a sense of humor and shared the vast wisdom.

This includes my Mother and Father—yogis at a time long before yoga was common or even accepted in America — and my sister . . .
— all of whom were my first teachers. To you I am grateful beyond measure. This is a unique year for the number **108** in our family . . .
my father's **108th** anniversary of birth is **2009.** I am grateful to my wife and two children who have inspired me over these years to keep my glass always somewhere between half-full and completely flowing over the brim.

As I developed and formulated the inspirations of my childhood, my first teacher — Paramahansa Yogananda— showered constant spiritual on our family. Then along came Yogi Bhajan; my teacher of the past forty years, who found me when I was just leaving childhood and taught me to take what was inside and mold it into being a teacher, a master, an adult, and yet forever, the curiously learning child. And to our dear friends the Dalai Lama, Sri Amma Bhagavan, and Anthony Robbins, who inspire and assist millions globally to invoke their Divine Presence, . . . we are eternally grateful.

A deep and constant gratitude to the Prophets and Avatars of every faith; the wisdom and teachings you have brought to this Earth — no matter how misinterpreted it might currently be — serves the collective human consciousness in ways beyond measure.

A particular thanks to the countless seekers and students throughout time — you challenge every moment of every teacher's world,
— to become the very best.

IV

A huge blessing to three major contributors* who worked directly on '108 Ways to Great Days'; this book is brought to life by their unique, spiritual and artistic talents.

— *Michael Sat Pavan Singh Newsom, the graphic artist and creative wizard/musician, devoted his heart to each and every artistic detail from cover to cover, and captured then drove the overall theme.

— *Kevin Hutchings, the C.O.O. of The Guru Singh Global Community, championed and edited the manuscript—with all its quirky stylistics-and kept it from getting lost amongst the other diamonds of our day to day campaigns.

— *Lisa Guru Deep Kaur Schiavello, the Art Director of The Guru Singh Global Community, keeps all of our quirkiness remaining on the point of our brand.

We are grateful to you the readers and journalists for participating with this spiritual technology.

We present '108 Ways to Great Days' with Great Sacred Love, Blessings, Prayer and Gratitude . . .

Sat Nam,
Guru Singh and Guruperkarma Kaur

Introduction

JOURNEY THROUGH JOURNALING

There are many ways to journal. The *process* used in this book is known as *Flash Journaling*. Flash Journaling conveys to the consciousness, information found in both the subconscious and the super-conscious minds. A profound method requiring only a few minutes each day, we recommend writing daily without breaking the pattern, to experience the depth of your views.

Flash Journaling is a "real-time" process; you are affected by it as you do it. It is also a reflective process that invites occasional review. Look back over your insights and gauge how you are progressing.

This is quite different from writing in a diary, different than jotting down a summary of events, or logging personal feelings. Flash Journaling transforms the *meme* in which you exist, that holds you in place as you attempt to grow. In order to see outside this mass conclusion, Flash Journaling drills into the core of your personal physical, psychological, emotional, and Spiritual DNA to bring up new possibilities.

With Flash Journaling, you stop telling your old stories for a moment and a new conversation opens up. You stop feeding the opinions that nourish the beliefs that cause the old conversation to define you. Suddenly there appears an innocent sense of ease where the old thoughts and opinions once held their positions. Flash Journaling is one of the keys, one of the tools, to cause this transformation.

Flash Journaling works as nature works:

- First find a quiet place where you can be undisturbed for a short time.

- Sit in a comfortable position with your eyes closed, focus on your breathing for a few moments and let your thoughts slow down as the pressures of the day drift away.

- Open this book—read the 'inspiration' from atop the left hand page, then write freely using as much of the two open pages as needed. You can come back and write again if you like.

- Steer clear from pre-scripted thoughts that analyze, structure and sort out the internal discussion, or attempt to predetermine the outcome. Just pour words onto the page; writing from the depth of your feelings with no interpretations. You will improve with practice.

- In a pure manner— you experience the experience of here 'n' now— described through the words flowing onto paper.
Past, present and future collide into this moment of journaling . . . deepening your understanding.

- The words of the **108** Inspirations will stimulate a response at a cellular level. These responses can be used to gain a compassionate advantage in a competitive world. This wisdom and mastery will manifest a compassionate counter-world.

NOTE:
You may notice unusual punctuation (the quirky style mentioned earlier), new words, and even apparent mis-spellings in this book.
It has all been used for a purpose, for a specific effect, and is well intended.
Language and punctuation are codes and are evolutionary processes of consciousness. At times, older rules must be reviewed and stretched or broken in order to open new thought doors, solicit new codes and present new perspectives.
Enter these doorways and pass through them with Joy.

What is your life's purpose as seen through the eyes of
this day?... this week?... this month?... and this year?
What are you mastering today?
this week?... this month? ...and this year?

Fearless Wisdom

Matter is the stage on which the story known as "creation" unfolds. How do you work with those forces that bond us?... How do you handle the pressure, the friction, the stress, and the tension? This is how your story is told.

Fearless Wisdom

Invest your time to master the body and brain as friends...
Your emotions will then embrace and serve you as family.

Fearless Wisdom

DAY 3

When you can't be the solution, at least be the compassion.

Fearless Wisdom

DAY 4

4

When we allow circumstances to govern our lives,—
life is seldom rewarding.
At that time we have become a passenger in our world.
Be the driver, not a passenger in the vehicle of your life . . .
then drive the road from *where* you are to *who* you are.

Fearless Wisdom

DAY 5

5

In life we are consistently surrounded by
a variety of characters, . . . each one bringing lessons.
It is never about the character with the lessons.
It is always about the lessons in the character.
Strike up the conversations that uncover the lessons.

Fearless Wisdom

The Human psyche has the unique ability to experience the reality of GOD.

108 Ways to Great Days !

Fearless Wisdom

Do not let life become the accumulation of "I'll do it tomorrow's".
Set your expectations as high as you can imagine,
then work daily to activate them.

Fearless Wisdom

It is good to be a fool, but not an idiot. The fool remains neutral and clear and does not make harsh judgments. The idiot may or may not make harsh judgments, but also -- never makes sense.

DATE: 108 Ways to Great Days !

Fearless Wisdom

If we avoid the pain along the road of our mission;
we can still fulfill the mission, but we will always repeat the pain.

Fearless Wisdom

DAY 10

Learn to learn the power of each lesson . . .
beyond the limitations of each fear,
without the pressure of each doubt . . .
within the blessings of each courageous moment.

DAY 11

DAY 11

Fearless Wisdom

A sk yourself: What are the thought-forms I generated today? . . .
Do they add or subtract from my vision of tomorrow?
Then determine the proper action to guarantee the vision.

DAY 12

DATE:

108 Ways to Great Days !

Fearless Wisdom

DAY 12

In the ocean of life we have waves, winds and rocks . . .
keep your bow facing the waves,
tactfully angle with the winds,
and steer clear of the rocks.

Fearless Wisdom

DAY 13

13

Allowing your feelings to become hurt when you are judged,
is but another way of expressing; 'I buy that'.
By being hurt, we are buying into what has been judged.

Fearless Wisdom

DAY 14

Act your age! . . .
ancient, eternal, compassionate, wise and fun-loving!

Fearless Wisdom

Honor GOD, the Mother and the Father,
by giving your body-vessel a standing ovation every morning.
Then, accept the massive grace and immortal authority
that dwells in each day.

DATE:

108 Ways to Great Days !

Fearless Wisdom

DAY 16

To be truly authentic and understanding of anything at all . . .
we must see beyond the space of this time,
and live beyond the time of this space.

DATE: 108 Ways to Great Days !

Fearless Wisdom

DAY 17

Our children do not look to us to make a dollar . . . they look to us to make a difference.

Fearless Wisdom

Bless the tiny ants of this world— going about their business in such a profoundly organized fashion-- they pay little attention to us except for our crumbs and sweets. They are in fact our 'Life-Keepers' . . .if we ruin this planet; they will still be here, the only ones left holding onto life itself . . . assigned to re-evolve us back to 'us' once again.

DAY 19

Fearless Wisdom

Make this a daily routine . . . stretch deep into your body glove and liberate the morning's doubt with love.

Fearless Wisdom

Intend to attend to each day as a gift.

DAY 21

DATE:

108 Ways to Great Days !

Fearless Wisdom

Doing unto others as you would have them do unto you is not a choice— it is an unwavering reality of our universe. Such is the 'law of the mirror' . . . giving back to *you*— exactly—what you give to *it*.

DAY 22

Fearless Wisdom

DAY 22

One by one, we have incorporated the Elements into our domain
—the Earth, the Water, the Fire, the Air and the Ether—
and now we are to master them.
Every day, pray and appreciate each one of them personally.

Fearless Wisdom

DAY 23

We cannot manage the emotions . . . yet with yoga and meditation, we are able to manage the glands and the organs of the body which create the emotions.

Fearless Wisdom

DAY 24

The path to Mastery is not the simple one,
and it is most certainly not the path of least resistance.

Fearless Wisdom

Create your defense without becoming defensive . . .
create your offense without becoming offensive.

DATE:

108 Ways to Great Days !

Fearless Wisdom

DAY 26

The immaculate combination of Spirit and matter
creates the truth of life . . . cherish it constantly.

DAY 27

DATE: 108 Ways to Great Days !

Fearless Wisdom

DAY 27

Tell your story often enough and you *become* your story.
The question you must ask is . . .
    Is your story the story you want to be?

Fearless Wisdom

DAY 28

The old ways of spiritual and religious education had teachers sequestered in hierarchies of exclusion. Wisdom was a proprietary commodity to be sacrificially earned. Today's *authentic* way of teaching is through inclusion, honoring wisdom as humanly inherent—though dormant— to be entrained and ignited.

Fearless Wisdom

Science has proven—love grows the brain.

DAY 30

Fearless Wisdom

In the competitive world there is a relentless push
to move you forward . . .
in the compassionate world there is wondrous inspiration
that draws you forward.

DAY 31

Fearless Wisdom

What magnificent experience can you offer GOD today?

Fearless Wisdom

DAY 32

To capture the impression of any great moment;
you must be soft enough to capture it,
and firm enough to hold it.

DATE: 108 Ways to Great Days !

Fearless Wisdom

DAY 33

If it happens *to* you, it happens *through* you . . .
we see through what we stand behind. The only way to
change the outer world is to change your inner agreement.

Fearless Wisdom

Never run to GOD . . . hold your Grace . . .
the Grace of GOD will run through you.

Fearless Wisdom

Be aware of the Earth's collective pain momentarily
and daily . . . . -- do not dwell in it monumentally,
but make a place in your heart for relieving it.

Fearless Wisdom

We are authorized to be whatever we imagine,
through the license of each breath.
Have a child's innocence . . . an adult's determination . . .
and then expect success.

Fearless Wisdom

DAY 37

I am not the doer . . . I am the mission.
GOD will do . . . what I envision.

Fearless Wisdom

DAY 38

Pass through darkness . . . and the light was always there.

DATE: 108 Ways to Great Days !

Fearless Wisdom

DAY 39

39

Once you remove the need to blame . . .
you create the cause to heal.

Fearless Wisdom

Exasperation, desperation and frustration are always within easy reach and deliver a known result. Inspiration, concentration and determination will take a bit longer to master, but will be worth the wait.

DAY 41

Fearless Wisdom

We have a choice to see what we are going through as either *overwhelming* or *understandable* . . . knowing you have such a choice is true power.

DAY 42

DAY 42

Fearless Wisdom

As there is a straw that breaks the camel's back . . . there comes a moment that can break through that which blocks you.

Fearless Wisdom

The only way to stop an argument is to stop arguing.

Fearless Wisdom

DAY 44

Do unto others as you would have others do unto you . . .
teach others to love you by loving your *self* as an example.

Fearless Wisdom

ach moment is alive . . . connecting to each moment
creates momentum. Any trepidation invested in a moment
is the power of momentum abandoned.

Fearless Wisdom

DAY 46

Use momentum to blaze new trails and embrace your flaws with courage.

Fearless Wisdom

Do not spend your life earning a living —
spend your life living the life you have already earned.

DAY 48

Fearless Wisdom

DAY 48

Manage your doubt . . .
do it with the same fierce commitment with which you
manage your debt.

Fearless Wisdom

DAY 49

Everything dies to be reborn as nighttime dies into dawn.

DATE:

108 Ways to Great Days !

Fearless Wisdom

DAY 50

In the face of danger, be a warrior . . .
In the face of ignorance, be a scholar . . .
In the face of sadness, be a friend . . .
In the face of chaos, be a mentor . . .
In the face of darkness, be a light . . .
In the face of joy, roll in it . . .

Fearless Wisdom

Sing with the elders and dance with the children.

Fearless Wisdom

Destiny is a choice to be made . . .
not a rule to be followed.

DAY 53

Fearless Wisdom

Fully experience any pain and the pain is over . . .
avoid the pain and the pain is waiting.

DAY 54

Fearless Wisdom

On the road of life; do not blame tires for going flat . . .
there is no one's fault in the scattered nails . . .
quickly change to your spare and joyously drive on.

Fearless Wisdom

Bees are not attracted to a bud—you have to blossom. Blossomed destiny equals the reason for life..

Fearless Wisdom

Expectations are not wantings . . .
they are knowings beyond knowing . . .
they are the deep unconscious forces that create our reality.
Get in touch with them, get to know them intimately,
and make them your friends.

Fearless Wisdom

A majority does not always define what is right—
it simply defines an opinion . . . quite loudly.

Fearless Wisdom

In the ancient scriptures it was written,
"There is no prayer more powerful
than the prayer of the mother."
The mother-child connection is the physical world vibrating
at the frequency of DNA . . . nothing can deflect this will.

DAY 59

Fearless Wisdom

DAY 59

The only value money has, is the trust or fear we give to it.
Develop your rewardability by working for value—not for a price.

DATE :

108 Ways to Great Days !

Fearless Wisdom

DAY 60

Competition is head to head—
Compassion is heart to heart.
We will remain in our competitive mire . . .
until our unconditional courage teams up with our pure desire.

DATE:

108 Ways to Great Days !

Fearless Wisdom

'Cour' is Latin for the heart . . .
and 'age' means time . . .
courage is a time of the heart.

DATE :

108 Ways to Great Days !

Fearless Wisdom

Every human is endowed with the capacity to create reality— take advantage of this human birthright.

Fearless Wisdom

Your needs will be met by the gratitude
that your needs will be met.

Fearless Wisdom

Allowing physical, emotional, mental, or spiritual pain to completely unveil its story is a meditative process. This is not dwelling in the pain — quite the opposite — this is connecting to the cause. Embrace the lesson and allow its cause to unravel and dissolve.

Fearless Wisdom

You *know* what you want, but you *get* what you expect.
Raise your expectations.

Fearless Wisdom

DAY 66

You are fortunate to be confident that the infinite will take care of it.

DAY 87

DATE:

108 Ways to Great Days !

Fearless Wisdom

DAY 67

67

I am who I am—that is that.
I am who you are looking back.
You are who I am — imagine that!

Fearless Wisdom

Be eternal . . . enter the space that is not yet occupied . . . then move into the space that does not yet exist.

Fearless Wisdom

The classic definition of education:
Exploring the unknown with enough courage to make all the mistakes that are required to turn the unknown into knowledge.

Fearless Wisdom

DAY 70

70

Don't get caught sneaking through your life. Turn over the newest leaves — open up to unknown spaces — live the life of being you.

DAY 71

Fearless Wisdom

When your goal is resolution—release judgment and engage trust.

DAY 72

Fearless Wisdom

DAY 72

72

It has taken billions of years to make preparations
for what we are now to accomplish in one lifetime . . .
such is the amazement of GOD's hand . . .
known to us as evolution.

Fearless Wisdom

DAY 73

onfusion is - rejecting what stands in the way of change,
but not yet possessing the strength to change it.

Fearless Wisdom

DAY 74

As long as you are embracing your dreams . . .
they will continue to awaken.
Enable these dreams to fulfill your demands with your supply.

DATE: 108 Ways to Great Days !

Fearless Wisdom

It is never too late to be what you might have been.
Give yourself the right to want the world you want.
Determine the why and you will get to the how.

Fearless Wisdom

DAY 76

Use food for nutrition, not for entertainment. Fear, as a tiny spice, is a great motivator... but a terrible diet.

Fearless Wisdom

How meaning-less our trials . . .
how meaning-full their lessons.
Life is a series of such lessons . . .
learn to learn your way through them.

DATE: 108 Ways to Great Days !

Fearless Wisdom

DAY 78

Allow the information of learning to enter a silent mind.

Fearless Wisdom

If someone is putting pressure on you — thank them for the workout — then enjoy how much stronger you feel.

DATE:

108 Ways to Great Days !

Fearless Wisdom

DAY 80

80

Every moment you forgive,
relieves suffering from the Earth. By experiencing,
not avoiding this pain, you heal the world of this pain.

DATE: 108 Ways to Great Days !

Fearless Wisdom

When you enter any room, make it your home—
then enable all others in the room to feel at home.
Don't try to fit in — you fit perfectly in you.

DAY 82

Fearless Wisdom

Live in the infinite gratitude
and the eternal consequence
of each moment.

DAY 83

Fearless Wisdom

You are not here to be approved of,
or to prove anything —
you are here to improve everything.

DAY 84

Fearless Wisdom

84

All life is lived within every single moment.
A moment is both an eternal and a temporal measure . . .
the quantum and the observed.

108 Ways to Great Days !

Fearless Wisdom

The measure of any moment has a quality of total flexibility. It can be the uniqueness of the temporal and the infinite possibilities of eternity. Use this flexibility to achieve your greatest power . . . your 'immortal authority'.

Fearless Wisdom

In the Quantum reality, observation is everything . . .
observation and expectations are siblings . . .
embrace them.

Fearless Wisdom

There is a relationship between a flaw and its cause. In today's world we obsess over the flaws, and causes are often ignored. This attention adds a charge to the cause, but does cure the flaw.

Fearless Wisdom

DAY 88

As your conscious awareness increases, not only do you notice more joys in this world, but you also notice more garbage. Can you handle this dichotomy? Can you stare down this 'devil' and remain inspired and loving?

Fearless Wisdom

At the end of any event, any process, any task, and any job . . . never resign . . . always transcend. Resignation is quitting . . . transcending on the other hand is a graduation.

Fearless Wisdom

DAY 90

As long as your story has someone else at fault, you are powerless to change the outcome.

Fearless Wisdom

Your existence is an unbroken river,
from the beginning before any beginning,
until after the end beyond any end.
The more you connect with this way, the more
your imaginings just show up. They were there all along . . .
the only thing that has changed is
your awareness of their existence.

DAY 92

Fearless Wisdom

When does your extreme schedule and busy lifestyle pattern become a reason, an excuse, or a distraction for the lack of personal fulfillment?

DAY 93

Fearless Wisdom

The reward from life comes when you are in touch
with both your destiny, and achieving your goals.
Learn — through your practice and your discipline —
to honor both . . .
this will open up your highest potential . . . the reward of joy.

DAY 94

Fearless Wisdom

Commitment has a promise to always re-commit . . .
it must be a fact and it must always be an act,
constant and consistent . . . renewed as a guarantee with
every breath. It is never optional, never allowed to die . . .
commitment is as valuable as life. With true commitment,
be on the lookout for miracles.

Fearless Wisdom

When the emotional body is transfixed
on an event that is no longer of service to you -
use the power of commitment and the consistency of discipline
to transpose, transmute, and transform the event.

Fearless Wisdom

Nothing on a Caterpillar is as fragile and vulnerable as the Butterfly's wings, but nothing else on the Butterfly allows such spectacular freedom.

Fearless Wisdom

When you present yourself with more than you can choose from, *that* is a choice . . . such a choice often fails, but remember, it was a choice, and you are authorized to make a different one.

Fearless Wisdom

earn the courage it takes to permit your 'self'
to become vulnerable and, at times, fragile . . .
then use this extremely sacred space to flourish in.

DAY 99

Fearless Wisdom

Patience is not sitting and waiting;
patience is sitting and knowing . . .
holding the space for the achievement that you trust will be.
However, patience, not accompanied by personal persistence,
is just wasting time, waiting for time.

DAY 100

Fearless Wisdom

If you teach others how to love you by loving your *self*, you give everyone the opportunity to experience love.

DATE:

108 Ways to Great Days !

Fearless Wisdom

DAY 101

When you find a wall blocking your plans,
kiss it, adore it, and look for the doorknob.
Remember: "If it happens *to* you, it happens *through* you",
and every wall in life has a door, and every door has a knob.
Turn the knob with clear intention and step through
into the world you have both earned to have and learned to have.

DAY 102

Fearless Wisdom

Each forgiveness recalibrates from
the moment you are, unto the infinity you are.

Fearless Wisdom

When you enter the realm of your immortal authority and begin thinking through the higher centers of your wisdom brain . . . the 'overwhelm' of your life, reduces down to child's play.

Fearless Wisdom

Pleasure is a feeling sought outside yourself . . .
happiness is a state of being found within you.
Happiness is your birthright, encoded directly into the DNA.
Maintaining a constant awareness of your universal authority
for being happy . . . is the key to being it.

DATE: 108 Ways to Great Days !

Fearless Wisdom

Continue to conjure up all the
original sensations of your vision,
never be turned away by the twists and turns of the path . . .
the river may bend, but it never loses sight of the ocean.

DATE:

Fearless Wisdom

Consistently and constantly evolve
to where the mind is clear . . . here, the clarity can
govern your world through inspiration, intuition, and
enthusiasm . . .rather than concern, struggle, and frustration.

DAY 107

DATE:

108 Ways to Great Days !

Fearless Wisdom

DAY 107

Upon awakening every morning . . . bow down,
in the deepest and humblest gratitude,
to the Infinite Divinity within you.

Fearless Wisdom

Made in the USA
Charleston, SC
25 November 2009